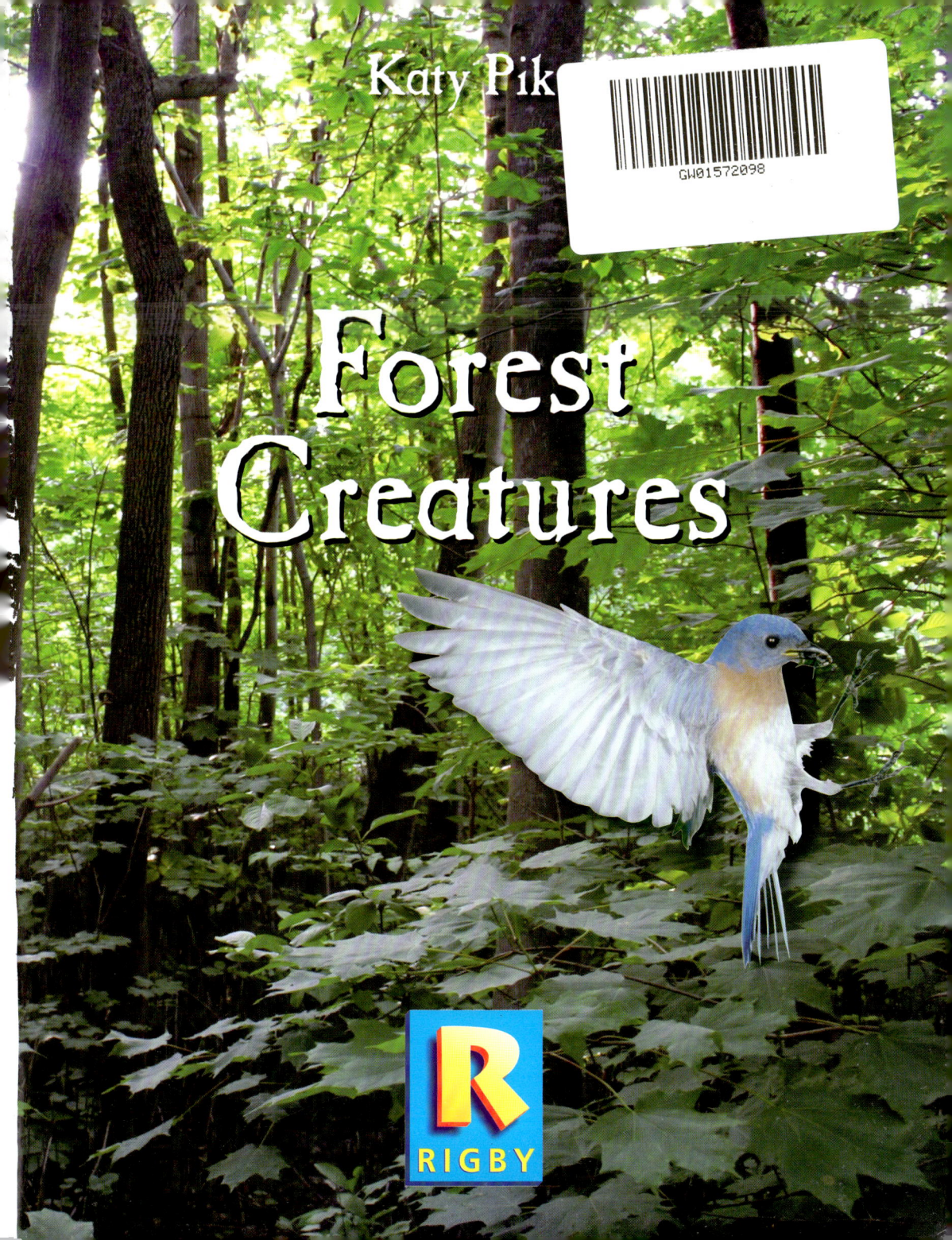

Katy Pike

Forest Creatures

Contents

Forests and Forest Creatures — 4

Pine Forests — 8

Rainforests — 12

Temperate Forests — 16

Dry Forests — 20

Glossary and Index — 24

Forests and Forest Creatures

In a forest, there can be thousands and thousands of trees. As well as trees, lots of other plants live in forests. Many different kinds of animals, birds and insects make their homes in the forest.

You wouldn't want to count all the trees in this pine forest!

There are many different kinds of forest in the world. Forests can grow in places that are cold or hot, and wet or dry. Different kinds of forests have different kinds of plants and animals.

This forest is in a hot, wet place. It is a rainforest.

World map

Forests can be very large. This map shows some of the biggest forests on Earth.

Large forests are shown in green on this map.

FACT!

Forests cover about one third of all the land on Earth.

Pine Forests

Pine forests grow in cold places. Pine trees can live in places that have lots of snow and rain. It is often dark in pine forests, because the trees grow close together.

Pine trees don't have leaves – they have needles. Pine needles are very thin. They can be quite sharp – almost like real needles!

pine needles

Pine trees have small seeds that grow inside pine cones. Animals such as squirrels like to chew pine cones and eat the seeds.

There are seeds inside this pine cone.

Pine Forest Animals

Many animals live in pine forests, including wolves, reindeer and moose.

This is a grey wolf.

Every year, reindeer lose their antlers and grow new ones.

Moose have large antlers too!

These owls are sitting on the branch of a pine tree.

Many birds live in pine forests too. Owls are birds of prey. This means that they kill and eat small animals and birds.

Rainforests

Rainforests grow in hot, wet places. There are rainforests in many different parts of the world, from South America to Australia.

FACT!
More than half of all the different kinds of animals and plants on Earth live in rainforests.

Rainforest trees often have large, flat leaves to soak up sunlight.

Rainforest plants often have brightly coloured flowers. The bright colours help birds and insects to see the flowers.

These rainforest flowers are called orchids.

Rainforest Animals

Many different kinds of animals live in the rainforest – from tiny animals such as frogs, to very large animals such as elephants.

This gorilla lives in a rainforest in Africa.

Orang-utans swing through the rainforest trees in South-East Asia.

Rainforest birds and animals are often very colourful. These parrots have brightly-coloured feathers. Their sharp beaks help them crack the hard shells of nuts in the forest.

Temperate Forest Animals

Many different kinds of animals live in temperate forests around the world.

This is a young deer. It has small antlers.

Skunks live in temperate forests in America.

Moles live in burrows under the ground.

Large birds such as eagles and small birds such as woodpeckers can live in temperate forests.

Eagles are birds of prey. They fly high above the forest.

Woodpeckers use their sharp beaks to tap on tree trunks. They are looking for bugs and insects to eat.

Dry Forests

Forests grow in hot, dry places around the world. In Australia, eucalyptus trees grow in the dry forests. Eucalyptus trees are also called gum trees.

Eucalyptus trees can grow very tall.

Eucalyptus trees have tough, oily leaves. The oil in the leaves means that the trees can easily catch fire.

This forest of eucalyptus trees is on fire.

Dry Forest Animals

Lots of unusual animals live in the dry forests of Australia.

This is a koala. Koalas live in eucalyptus trees. They like to eat the leaves.

Sugar gliders live in dry forests. They can glide between the trees.

Many kinds of parrots live in the dry forests of Australia too.

These pink and grey parrots like to sit high up in the eucalyptus trees.

Glossary

deciduous trees that lose their leaves in the autumn

temperate weather that is neither very hot nor very cold

Index

beech trees 16
birch trees 16
deciduous trees 17
deer 10, 18
eagles 19
eucalyptus trees 20, 21, 22, 23
flowers 13
gorilla 14
koalas 22
moles 18
moose 10
orang-utan 14
orchids 13
owls 11
parrots 15, 23
pine cones 9
pine needles 9
pine trees 8, 9
reindeer 10
skunks 18
sugar gliders 22
wolves 10
woodpeckers 19